AWAKENING TO AWE AND WONDER

Helene King

Published by Mark Gyde
First Published in Great Britain in 2017
Copyright © Helene King

The right of Helene King to be identified as the author of this work has been asserted by him in accordance with the
Copyright, Designs and Patents Act 1988.

All rights reserved. No part of this publication may be reproduced, stored in a retrieval system, or transmitted in any form or by any means, without the prior written permission of the author, nor be otherwise circulated in any form of binding or cover other than that in which it is published and without a similar condition being imposed on a subsequent purchaser.

Unless otherwise stated Scriptures are taken from the Holy Bible, New International Version.
Copyright © 1973, 1978, 1984 by International Bible Society.
Used by permission of Hodder & Stoughton.
All rights reserved.

ISBN 978-0-9567792-7-4

Cover design by Trevor Mason
Cover photograph © Mark Gyde

"Wonder is the Beginning of Wisdom"

Socrates, a Greek philosopher born in 469BC

ACKNOWLEDGEMENTS

My grateful thanks to James and Denise Jordan, of Fatherheart Ministries, for imparting to me the beginnings of the revelation that Almighty God is my Father which has caused me to have my heart awakened to see people and even creation very differently. Through their ministry they have awakened me to see Life in a very different way.

My thanks to Julia Mackel for helping me to edit this book, and to Mark Gyde for his friendship, comforting presence, and for his help in pulling this book together and for his belief in me.

Thanks to Trevor and Linda Galpin for their encouragement on the journey.

My thanks to Mark Pecqueur who has journeyed with me for many years.

And finally, my thanks to everyone with whom I have been, and still am, on the journey with, and who has enriched my life in so many ways.

FOREWORD

Helene King is my sister and my friend.

I first met Helene in a large meeting while I was praying for and ministering to a long line of people. It was a dramatic moment.

Since then Helene has been an integral part of Fatherheart Ministries and a mother and inspiration to so many of us.

Although Helene's journey is akin to a mystic's, her many years of ministry to young people (largely from housing schemes in Edinburgh) have shown her to have a hands-on ministry in the real world and to be a demonstration of the likeness of Jesus. She is well acquainted with the brokenness and pain of the human race. The Love of God, the Father flows from her in real depth to all who come across her path.

You will grow from the influence of the Spirit that leads, strengthens and teaches Helene King.

James Jordan
Fatherheart Ministries, New Zealand

INTRODUCTION

This book contains the ponderings of my heart which are sometimes difficult to explain, because I believe that spiritual things are tasted before they are understood, when words are often hard to find.

I will describe my awakening to awe and wonder at the extravagant grace and love of God the Father.

It is very difficult, and perhaps even impossible, to differentiate or discern between the love and grace of God.

In 1993 I was a very good Christian. I remember the day as if it was yesterday. I was sitting in my living room reading my bible and I had decided to read the little book of Titus that Paul the Apostle wrote. I like reading slowly to really understand what is being spoken about. I got to chapter three, verse five, where Paul says, *'He saved us, not because of righteous things we had done, but because of His mercy.'*

It is one thing to read the bible, but it is another thing when the bible reads you.

I was so excited to read this passage that I ran into the kitchen speaking into the air and into myself. Perhaps this is what God's 'grace' must be.

Much of the Christian church at that time was talking about the word 'grace'. We use words but often we don't know what they really mean. So I decided to go to the Christian bookshop where I lived in Edinburgh and buy every book I could find about grace to give me a greater understanding of what this word 'grace' meant.

I read those books many times and enjoyed them, but they did not give me the deeper understanding of what the word really meant.

As this book gently unfolds, I will explain more of the depth of this.

I am one of those people who like to look at the opposite of something to fully understand what that something means. So, I thought to myself, what book in the bible speaks about the opposite of 'grace'?

I was moved to read the book of Galatians, which we find in the New Testament. In this book we find Paul, the Apostle, writing to the Church in Galatia, and in chapter three, he begins, *'You foolish Galatians! Who has bewitched you? Before your very eyes Jesus Christ was clearly portrayed as crucified. I would like to learn just one thing from you: Did you receive the Spirit by the works of the law, or by believing what you heard?'*

What is Paul saying? Is he saying, 'you knew the truth, so why are you living by rules and regulations?'

I continued studying the whole letter to the Galatian church because in my heart I was searching for a greater understanding of what 'grace' really is. If what I read in Titus is true that, *'He saved us, not because of any righteous thing we had done, but because of His mercy,'* then there is nothing we need to do to earn it.

I realised for most of my Christian life I had been living by rules and regulations in order to make Him love me more, but as I studied and meditated I realised that all I needed to do was to accept that I was accepted.

I really enjoyed the study, but I came to something that really puzzled me in Galatians chapter three, verse twenty-six, which reads *'you are all sons of God through faith in Christ Jesus'* (NIV 1984). This verse is talking about sonship, and I must admit I did not understand it. I struggled with it for a long time, but eventually I got to the point of just letting it go and moved on to study the rest of the book.

Many of us just take the written word on the page literally and assume that because the bible says it, it must be true. But I have come to understand that there are three levels of scripture. The first is the written word on the page; the second is who wrote the passage and what was going on at the time; the third level is where it gives understanding and imparts life to the reader.

In 2003 I was in Toronto Airport Christian Fellowship Church in Canada, with my friends

Graeme and Julia Mackel, because I was very drawn to the incredible move of the Holy Spirit which was happening there at that time.

While I was there, I heard that a man called James Jordan from New Zealand, who leads Fatherheart Ministries, was speaking at a meeting in the church one evening. I was a bit like Paul who said he felt compelled by the Holy Spirit. That was what happened to me. I felt compelled to go and hear this man speak. I had never met the man or even heard him speak before.

An incredible thing happened that evening. James Jordan was speaking on this very passage of scripture in Galatians that I had struggled with ten years before. As he spoke, I received an understanding which was like a light beginning to dawn inside me. This study on sonship that I mentioned earlier has nothing to do with gender, and I began to come into an understanding of what sonship really means. I have come to realise that God is my Father, and this has changed everything for me.

At the beginning of Romans chapter eleven we find Paul asking a question, *'did God reject His people?'* and He answers *'by no means, I am an Israelite myself: a descendent of Abraham from the tribe of Benjamin. God did not reject His people whom He foreknew'.* Also in verse five of Romans chapter eleven Paul goes on to say, *'so too, at the present time there is a remnant chosen by 'grace'. And if by 'grace', then it cannot be based on works. If it were, 'grace' would no longer be 'grace'.*

Now I do not know much about the remnant of Israel, which is what this passage is talking about, and it is not what I want to look at just now. Paul's point and emphasis is on the 'grace' of God.

God did not reject His people. He chose them by His 'grace', and if He chose them by 'grace' it cannot be based on works, because if it was, 'grace' would no longer be 'grace'.

The incredible thing is that we can do nothing, absolutely nothing, to deserve God's 'grace'; it is pure graciousness, or 'grace' would not be 'grace'. All we are asked to do is to surrender to this, His extravagant 'grace'.

God's love is never determined by a worthy object of His love, but only by being true to who God is in Himself.

In the Christian Church of which I am part and love, I find that we (and I include myself) spend so much time and energy arguing over systems of belief and points of doctrine, and trying to prove who is right and who is wrong, who is in and who is out, that we can end up with a black and white religion and overlook what is more important: the awe and mystery of God, of Almighty God who is our Father.

We are not called to defend the truth, but to live it. I have discovered that whatever we believe in our heart will determine how we live.

If we see God as harsh and judgmental, then that is what we will impart to others. It seems to me that if we want to judge people then we will look for a judgmental God. If we want to reap vengeance on people then we will justify our actions by looking for a vengeful God.

But if we see God as our Father, as a God of love and mercy and grace and compassion, then we will find it easy to love others, even our enemies, and, dare I say it, even ourselves.

We use so much of our emotional, psychological and physical energy trying to get through every day instead of living. When we live that way, we can end up having very little peace, and we exhaust ourselves when we start trying to prove that we are right and keep comparing ourselves to those around us.

I often think of Peter, one of Jesus' disciples, who was an incredible guy, but who struggled with the same insecurities that you and I struggle with.

In John's gospel chapter twenty-one, verses fifteen to twenty-five, we read of the resurrected Christ cooking fish on the shore of the sea of Galilee when He calls Peter over and begins to reinstate him after his denial of being a follower of Jesus. Three times Jesus says to Peter 'feed my sheep', and I think it is a beautiful example of Jesus' affirmation of him.

Peter, being Peter, happened to turn and see the disciple Jesus loved walking along and he says, *'Lord, what about him?'* (verse twenty-one).

John had nothing to do with Peter's denial of Jesus, or of Jesus' reinstatement of Him, but Peter manages to take the focus off himself and on to John. He says, 'well what about him?' Jesus' answer is, as it is to all of us, 'what is that to you? You must follow me' (verse twenty-two).

We will never live from our true selves until we have peace with who we really are as sons and daughters of our Father. We also need to have courage to face our own shadow side, which we all have, and when we face it, and own up to it, we begin to realise His love for us even then.

Proverbs chapter fourteen, verse thirty, says, '*A heart at peace gives life to the body, but envy rots the bones*'. I have discovered in my journey through life that transformed people transform people, and I wonder if this kind of transformation is like a dance where we begin to experience a Oneness with the Godhead and get caught up in this flow of movement that brings us into a harmony. With this flow we begin to find that as we move into this that there is no striving, and it brings us into a place of rest.

LIVING LIFE

There has been a lot of talk over the past few years about 'catching the next wave', the next move of the Spirit. And although I love this, I sense a danger, where we are looking ahead for something to happen and not finding Him in the here and now, in the present moment. The reality is that He says in Hebrews chapter thirteen, verse five, *'Never will I leave you, never will I forsake you.'*

Our Father has not abandoned us and gone to reside somewhere else. Moses found Him in the wilderness when he took time to see the bush burning and heard God's voice speak to him (Exodus chapter three).

Jacob found Him when he awoke from his sleep in the desert and he said, I think in a voice of amazement, 'surely God was in this place and I never knew it.' (Genesis chapter twenty-eight)

We have had many moves of God over the centuries. For example, we had a strong move of Martin Luther, born in 1483, a German professor of theology and a seminal figure in the Protestant Reformation. We had an incredible move of the Holy Spirit in Azuza Street, Los Angeles, which began the Pentecostal movement which was led by William J. Seymour, an African American preacher.

Then in my lifetime we had an incredible move when the Holy Spirit fell in Toronto Airport Christian Fellowship, which birthed many Partner in Harvest Churches, and also many Catch the Fire Churches, and these are all over the world.

Wonderful, wonderful times.

With regard to catching the next wave of revival, which is what the Church all over the world was talking about a few years ago, there is something that draws me, because I love the sea and all its moods.

The sea can be quiet and calm but also quite forceful. I find that what God the Father is doing in the world today is revealing His love to us, which makes us face our pain but not in a forceful way. I would prefer to be in a deep place in the ocean rather than in the crashing of the waves where my feet are not even on the ground; not on the sandy bottom, but where I just go with the flow, the flow of the Holy Spirit, and get carried along and then begin to enter into the joy of being involved in what He is doing. This begins to awaken us to see the beauty all around with an awe and wonder that causes us to gasp with the thrill of being alive. I am also beginning to understand Saint Irenaeus, who was an early Church Father and was born in the second century. He said, 'The glory of God is man fully alive.'

William Wallace was a Scottish knight, and one of the main leaders during the wars of Scottish independence. He was asked just before he was executed, in 1305, 'Are you not afraid to die?' He said, 'All men die, but few men really live.' How true that is, if we only knew it.

I remind myself on a regular basis not to lose out on this gift of life, because I am discovering that some people never live at all.

The source of all this life is within the Godhead, as the Father gives to the Son, and the Son to the Spirit. It is a giving and receiving from one to the other in perfect harmony. It is like a flow of movement. It's like a dance.

If we don't allow ourselves to get caught up in this flow of movement within the Trinity as the Father gives to the Son and the Son to the Spirit, an eternal flow, then we will try to become victorious Christians and try to do it all by ourselves. We will then impose on ourselves and others, rules and regulations that lead to burnout and exhaustion. There is no fun in it, and we lose our joy. Therefore, there is no glory for God, our Father, when we do not become fully alive and appreciate that the life we have is a gift.

I believe what John O'Donahue, an Irish Priest and Poet, said, 'The greatest sin is the unlived life.'

Life is a gift given to us to enjoy and even amidst pain and suffering there is still a beauty to see if the eyes of our heart are open.

The only way our Father can break through all the rules we impose on ourselves is an awakening to His incredible 'grace'.

'Grace' is God's magnificent way of releasing us from all the prisons we have put ourselves in and all the chains we have bound ourselves up with. We use all our effort to pull ourselves up when we are down, because we have obeyed all the rules. What this does is to make us very self-righteous and we put ourselves on a higher level, a higher pedestal than other people, and when we do that we are inviting ourselves to fall.

In the book of Acts chapter seventeen, verse twenty-six we read that when Paul is speaking in Athens, not to Jews, not to Christians but to Greek-speaking people, he said, *'From one man (Adam, which means mankind) He made every nation of men that they should inhabit the whole earth; and he determined the times set for them and the exact places where they should live.'* (NIV 1984) This verse has changed how I see people and the world. I am realising that the very breath that went into Adam has also gone into every single one of us. So when I look at someone I do not see if they are black or white, rich or poor, or whatever country or race they come from. I see the divine spark that is in every human being.

This opens us up to experience all of the gifts that our Father wants to bestow on us. We then begin to awaken to the extravagant 'grace' of the Father, as He gives to us freely with no expectation of return. If there was any expectation of payback, it would then not be 'grace'.

Grace is the free bounty and benevolence of God to each one of us; as we grow in it we find that it is God Himself we want more than anything that He gives us. The focus then is on the Giver not the gifts.

Without 'grace' for ourselves and for other people we end up with all our focus being on ourselves, and all we see are our own hurts.

'Grace' can make us feel powerless, because before we knew His 'grace' we had the understanding that if we did all these right things for God we would then earn His favour. It would then be in our control or in our power to earn His favour.

Accepting 'grace' can make us feel poor and empty, and even useless, because we are admitting our vulnerability and the fact that we need Him. It is our reliability on God as our Father that changes us.

We can be big and strong and do it all ourselves, or we can become like a child and admit our helplessness and our need of Him.

If Jesus Christ, the Son of God, could do 'nothing by Himself', as it says in John chapter five, verse nineteen, why is it that we think we can conquer the world by ourselves?

So a question arises: 'Who wants His 'grace'?' I believe it is people who have need of His unconditional love.

When we can accept 'grace' we find that there is no room for judgement, because we begin to see the world through different eyes. And I believe that the eyes we are speaking of here are the eyes of our heart.

Living in 'grace' we begin to see the beauty that is all around us all the time, and we begin to find that we want to live a spirituality of letting go. Philippians chapter two, verses five to seven, says *'in your relationships with one another, have the same mindset as Christ Jesus: Who, being in very nature God, did not consider equality with God something to be used to his own advantage; rather, He made Himself nothing by taking the very nature of a servant.'* The King James Version of the bible says that He 'made Himself of no reputation'.

Could it be that as we go deeper in our walk with God we can get to the place where we do not want to grasp or cling to anything, even our reputation. This is how I want to live.

I wonder if we as Christians are so busy trying to hold ourselves up, that we need to let go of clinging to things so we can then find that He is holding us. We find that we are not in control, and that our weakness is really strength.

I hope that you like me, but if you don't, it will not destroy my world because I am beginning to find out who I really am, as a daughter of Almighty God, not based on what others think of me. I am coming to the place where I don't want to cling to my reputation or even my possessions, because when we see everything as our objects for our personal consumption, including, dare I say it, religion, it becomes a way to advance ourselves. Yet Christianity is about taking a lower place.

In everything Jesus said and did He gave glory to His Father. For us to become like Jesus Christ we need a spirituality of 'letting go'.

When all we want to do is to advance ourselves it does not transform us, and it is not a way of loving God or loving our neighbours. It does not bring glory to our Father.

Sometimes within Christian culture, we have the idea that things are there for me. They are, of course they are, but the danger comes when something becomes an object for our consumption; our focus is on our worthiness. This is not the Gospel. It is like going out for a meal with friends and we expect that we should be the centre of attention; so we talk louder, and laugh louder so that everyone's attention will be on 'me'.

Everything that Jesus said and did pointed to the Father; He took no glory for Himself. In John chapter eight, verse fifty-four, we read Jesus speaking *'if I glorify myself, my glory means nothing. My Father, whom you claim as your God, is the one who glorifies me.'*

MY EXPERIENCES IN CYPRUS

For many years I pastored CityLife, an inner-city children's ministry in Edinburgh, Scotland.

When I retired from pastoring CityLife Ministries, I went to Cyprus for a sabbatical because I wanted creation to wash my soul. Why was this? Was my soul dirty? Maybe it was.

Whatever the reason, that is what I wanted.

Whilst in Cyprus I spent time practising to be fully present. At first I practised looking at a flower, just to begin to really see. The next day I went out again to look at the same flower, but it had died. Along the hedge, a little way down, there was another flower, and I realised that without death there is no resurrection.

I have come to a deep realisation that we can make changes in a day, but it takes months, years, even a lifetime to work through the transformation. Perhaps it is even an ongoing process. 2 Corinthians chapter three, verse eighteen, says we *'are changed into the same image from glory to glory, even as by the Spirit of the Lord.'* (King James Version)

However, when we take time to stop and listen to the inner voices, we begin to find out who we really are.

There is a great difference between an inner journey and an inward one.

An inner journey is very important and very healthy. Even praying in a place of quiet without words is entering in to an inner journey. But an inward journey looks only at ourselves and our needs. You could say introspection.

I read somewhere about an American travelling in Africa who hired a guide to lead him through the jungle to a remote village. In the middle of the afternoon the guide stopped and began to rest, and the American asked why. The answer was 'we have travelled very fast and must allow time for our souls to catch up with our bodies'.

Some years ago I had a caravan by the beach near Dunbar in Scotland. One day whilst shopping in this small town I found a museum which was dedicated to John Muir, the conservationist, and I found in this museum something that he had written which really grabbed me.

> 'Go to the church of nature,
> Let the tired and worn go out,
> Go, drop whatever stops you.
> Go, go, go to the beauty of life that is free and open to everyone.
>
> Go and just be there in it, as part of it.
> In nature there are higher lands of the mind.

May I jump the boulders into myself.

There is an adventure in every ray of light.
There is a calling to me to get as near to
the heart of the world as I can.'

This understanding has been growing in me, and when I lived in Cyprus for a while, I had a real desire to go on a spiritual journey. Two friends, Geoff and Sylvia Hill, drove me to the north of Cyprus, which is the Turkish part of the island, to visit Barnabas's tomb, one of the disciples of Jesus.

I loved the journey and visiting the tomb, but nothing touched my heart except for when we drove alongside a mountain called Five Finger Mountain, and this blew me away to such an extent that I wrote a poem about it:

Five Finger Mountain (The Greeks call it Pentadactylos)

There is something about the mountains that draws my soul
There is a beauty in the hills where I can experience the air blowing on my face that brings refreshing to my tired spirit.

I can look at the hills, and as I focus and become fully present with my whole attention on them.
Not thinking of the past or worrying about tomorrow in this broken world

I can see the mountains have expressions,
as if they have a face.

Walking at night with my head lifted up
I can see the world of creation at play.
As I look at beauty all around me,
I realise that my Father is extravagant.

An extraordinary and extravagant Father
has given me the sight and sound of the
morning stars singing together,
And me, as His child, dancing for joy.

In this environment there is a healing balm
A health that is incredibly real and natural
and alive.

There is a health and vitality that is awake
And as we become part of it,
It begins to awaken us in the deepest part
of who we are.

The Holy Spirit is continually writing on the
landscape of nature's beauty, that is alive and
living and free.

There is something about being immersed in the
beauty of the world that is wanting to speak to us.
Something that goes deeper than words.

The beginning of my understanding is that there is
a language deeper than words, and this began
one day when I was ministering in Finland for the
first time. As I was sharing, the man who had

invited me, Pekka Daniel Rimpelainen, who leads Fatherheart Ministries there, said to me through an interpreter. 'Helene, although I speak no English, I understand what you are saying.'

That to me is incredible and started me on this journey that I am still on, to begin to commune with God our Father, with people, and even with creation itself without the spoken word.

There is a deeper connection of heart and mind that words cannot convey.

I am so grateful to Pekka Daniel for helping me to see that there is a way of connection and Oneness that goes deeper than anything else.

Rumi was a poet and a theologian, born in 1207 in Iran; he said, 'the quieter you become, the more you are able to hear'.

There is a Voice that doesn't use words.

There is a kind of communion with nature and with the One who created all things.

I believe that prayer is sitting in the silence until it silences us.

This is what I started to experience in Cyprus. I owe so much to this island because while I was there I came to a much deeper realisation of who I am as a child on this earth. I am so grateful to Gabrielle who is the owner of the Grande tavern in

Peyia. I began to call this my Cypriot office. I would often meet with friends there to talk about the deep issues of life.

Also while living in Cyprus I was again sitting in my garden and I noticed some of the plants dying, and as I walked around these plants I found that the watering hose was not connected. It made me think that when we are not connected to the One who is the source of all life, we die spiritually.

My prayer is that the eyes of our hearts become uncovered and the ears of our hearts are opened to see and hear the wonder of God that is around us all the time.

Someone said 'may we begin to hear the rocks trembling in response to the rolling waters, making a music that our hearts are longing to hear'.

Robert Fripp, an English guitarist, born in 1946, said 'music is the cup that holds the wine of silence'.

Whether we hear it or not, the rocks are crying out and the waters are making music. If we can hear this deep within, it makes a music that stills and enlivens our soul.

Perhaps this is what it means in Romans chapter eight, verse twenty-two, where we read that *'the whole creation has been groaning.'*

All the air has a rhythm and a sound like music playing in perfect harmony.

Rumi also said 'we have fallen into the place where everything is music'.

I love that, because I believe that I have heard, in a small way, the song, the dance, the rhythm, the tune, that is playing all the time. It has one desire. That we would hear it, and as we begin to hear it, it brings us into harmony with the dance of heaven.

It is also what brings us into connection with others who are beginning to hear the tune. They may not know much about Christianity, but from the way they live their lives, there is no doubt that they are beginning to hear it. I am discovering that if I become harsh and judgmental, I am out of harmony with what is going on around me all the time. .... HIGH BEAMS, VERSUS ATTRACTIVE LIGHT

So the question comes. What is it we are beginning to hear? From my own experience the start of hearing this rhythm came through the beginning of having a revelation deep in my heart that my Father just happens to be Almighty God; He loves me and He is the creator of all things which He has given me to enjoy.

In the book of Ecclesiastes chapter one, verse eight we read *'the eye never has enough of seeing, nor the ear its fill of hearing'*. Perhaps the writer of Ecclesiastes is talking about seeing and hearing the mystery of awe and wonder of God which is around us the whole time. It is this revelation that our Father is bringing to our hearts.

Coming into the beginning of knowing that Almighty God is my Father has made me see the world through very different eyes.

Nature has been seen for thousands of years by people as God's first book. For me it took a revelation of God as my Father to bring me to a much quieter place within myself to actually see it.

Abraham Joshua Heschel was a Polish born American rabbi and a leading Jewish theologian, born in 1907. He said 'I did not ask for success, I asked for wonder.' This is what I want more than anything.

One day, while I was staying in Cyprus, I was taking three dogs for a walk because their owners were working. Each dog had a different length of lead and as I was walking, one dog went to the left and the other two went to the right; I came face to face with a lamp-post, and I thought, 'which way now?' I just started to laugh, with the joy of being alive. When I got the dogs organised, I continued walking and I noticed a tiny lizard on the side wall of one of the houses. I stood and looked at it for a long time and I thought, 'I don't know if this little lizard has any purpose in life except to eat flies. Then I thought, 'but my Father created it and I don't think it worries about anything.' So I decided to learn to live like this little lizard, without worrying about life. Why? Because, as it says in Luke 12:25 chapter twelve, verse twenty-five: *'who of you by worrying can add a single hour to your life?'* → Not one!

A few years ago I moved house and I found a journal with a poem that I had written when I was at Toronto Airport Christian Fellowship (TACF). While I was there, I experienced the thickness of the weight of the presence of the Holy Spirit.

Many people attended TACF and I had a longing to be seen through this gigantic maze of people. A question began to arise within me? Does anyone see me in the vast crowds of people on the earth?

Here is the poem I wrote about Bartimaeus:

Begging Bowl

On a hot and dusty road
Blind Bartimaeus sat
Outside the gate of Jericho
Upon his dusty mat.

His clothes were torn,
His heart forlorn,
His heavy load he had always borne.

His begging bowl was in his hand
But no one stopped
No one seemed to mind.

No one seemed to notice
No one seemed to care

They all passed by with a frozen stare.

But today his heart is very excited
He has heard the claims the people recited
That the Son of David was coming this way
Would He pass by with that frozen stare?

Although he never could see the folk stare
He always felt that it was there
Perhaps this man would look at him
And see the pain that was deep within.

Ah, here He comes
He hears the voices
There is quite a crowd
You can tell by the noise.

His heart begins to pound and beat
As he hears the sound of approaching feet
O Son of David have mercy on me,
I want to see, O I want to see.

I want to see your loving gaze
I want to be seen through this gigantic maze

I believe Lord Jesus that you have all power
And it's on me that I want it to shower
Your hand of healing
Your love divine
To touch my eyes
My heart set on fire.

> Bartimaeus Lord you set free
> O do the same I beg you to me.
> My cloak throw off with great delight
> And then serve you with all my might.

As I read my poem all these years later, I realised how lonely I had always felt. I have begun to understand how much my childhood had shaped me as a person. This was not my parents fault. They could never give to me what they had never received themselves.

This root of loneliness within me began when my dad broke his spine playing football, and he was in hospital for a long time. I grew up during this time with an absent father and this somehow shaped the belief that God as my Father was also not present with me and was somewhere far away, not just to meet my needs but to give me the fathering love that I so needed as a little girl.

How our earthly mother and father are to us, or what we perceive them to be, can form our view of what God the Father is also like.

It was not my father's fault.

I believe the time we are living in is a prophetic time in world history where God is revealing Himself as Father. As we come into this understanding we can begin to live in the 'glorious freedom' (Romans chapter eight, verse twenty-one)

In the year 2000 when I was in TACF, again at a conference, there was a woman called Judith McNutt speaking, and she said, 'Have you ever heard God call your name?'

My response was 'No. God I don't think you see me among the vast crowd of people on the earth.' Feeling lost is not about where you are going, but where you are.

I felt lost among the six thousand people in the meeting. So I began to ask God to say my name.

There was a popular song out at that time, and one of the lines in the song was 'Say my name, say my name, say my name.' So I began throughout the day just singing that one line, again and again. 'Say my name, say my name, say my name.'

Also at that time in my life I was pastoring CityLife Ministries in Edinburgh with lots of young people. Two children, who were brothers in the ministry, Stephen and Stuart Kenny, thought it would be a good idea to nominate me for an award given to people who work with young people. The award is called the BT Childline Award and I won the award in the year 2000; it was presented by the Duchess of Kent HRH. The event was hosted by Esther Rantzen, a well-known television presenter.

It was an incredible experience when I was presented with the award, because God, my Father, said to me 'you wanted Me to say your name and because I am proud of you, I want to say it publicly.'

In the year 2009 I retired from pastoring. A wise friend said to me 'do nothing for six months after retiring because you will hit something that is within you'. He said 'your identity is in Christ but your functional identity is in what you do; when you are not doing that any more you will hit something that is within you'.

I thought about what he said but laid it aside as I had no understanding what that would mean. A very kind friend, John MacLennan, offered to treat me to a six-month sabbatical anywhere in the world, so I chose Cyprus because it is warm, it is by the Mediterranean sea, and I love the sea and all its moods. While I was living in Cyprus, my family came out to visit me, and after they left I hit a depth of loneliness that I had never experienced to that degree before.

When this began to happen I heard the voice of my heavenly Father say 'Helene, you have run from facing this all your life. Sit with it'. So I did not phone a friend or watch the television or even read a book. All I did was walk during the day and go to sleep at night.

Some years later I remember speaking to my good friend Denise Jordan, about what I had been going through, and she said 'the problem is when you are going through something like this you don't know when it is going to end.' Such a wise thing to say, and so true.

There were many days and nights where I experienced the darkness of loneliness that at times I thought I was going mad. One night I remember walking and walking, and then suddenly something changed. I looked up to the sky and it had become like black velvet and the stars were so bright, it was difficult to look at them. I do not know what happened after that. I don't know if I was lifted up amongst the stars and the black velvet sky or that the stars and sky came down upon me. All I know is one thing, that I began to say, without any process of reasoning 'this is my Father's world, and I belong'. I have never struggled with loneliness again. I heard someone say that loneliness is where no one knows who you are. I think it is more than that. Denise Jordan says that loneliness is a disconnection from the heart. I believe that loneliness is when our heart is not connected to the One who is the source of life.

I have learned about loneliness and I have come to realise that you do not always need to sit outside in the dark, but I am discovering that if you want to see the stars, darkness is required. God is light and this light seems to shine even in the darkness.

Sometimes in the pain of our journey through life we must enter the darkness (not the darkness of demonic things) before we can see the light.

How did the wise men find Jesus? They followed a star (Matthew chapter two, verse two). The light had never been far away.

Vincent Van Gough, a famous artist, born in 1853 in the Netherlands, said 'looking at the stars always makes me dream.'

The place of suffering in my own life which was revealed in Cyprus, and the emptiness I experienced, I believe has led me to coming under the incredible mystery of God. Seeing the stars as I had never seen them before was the beginning of me being able to see the mountain behind the mountain, an invisible strand that is really there all the time. It is not that there is another kingdom because that implies separation; it would be saying that God is somewhere else, but He is not. He is fully present, right here, right now. I believe I was beginning to be aware of the loneliness in Toronto when I wrote the poem about Bartimaeus, but I did not fully recognise it then.

I believe that deep within us we have layers or depths of pain. And God in His grace allows us to face what He feels we are able to face.

The loneliness I felt when Judith McNutt said 'have you ever heard God call your name', then the loneliness I experienced in Cyprus. I have come to understand it is when we don't fight that these things are revealed to us and we find that He is going deeper still.

It is because of His mercy that He goes deeper and has taken us deeper. We often cannot handle great depth all at once. This experience has begun to open me up to the mystery of all life being like a sacrament where God breaks through the ordinary everyday things of life with a glory, a weight of the heaviness of His presence, that totally surprises us.

FURTHER REFLECTIONS

A British poet, Minnie Louise Haskins, born in 1875, wrote the following

> 'I said to the man who stood at the gate of the year
> Give me a light that I may tread safely into the unknown
> And he replied … go out into the darkness and put your hand into the hand of God
> That shall be to you better than light and safer than a known way.'

This was spoken by a British monarch, King George VI in his Christmas 1939 broadcast, with the country facing the uncertainty of war. (I was born in April 1938, so perhaps this is why it means so much to me, that I believe it to be true.)

God is light and that light would shine in the darkness of the world, giving us a better vision, where the light on our broken world seems to be growing dim.

Jesus said in John chapter twelve, verse fifty *'whatever I say is just what the Father has told me to say'*. JOHN 12:52

Jesus said in John chapter fourteen, verse eighteen *'I will not leave you as orphans; I will come to you.'* These must then be the direct words JOHN 14:18

of the Father, our Father. He is the ever present
God with us all the time.

[margin note: Eph 1:18]

Perhaps it is us who have lost the ability to see,
when all we see is darkness all around us. We see
these things through the eyes of the heart.
Ephesians chapter one, verse eighteen says '*I
pray that the eyes of your heart may be
enlightened in order that you may know the hope
to which He has called you'*. Proverbs chapter [margin note: 4:23]
four, verse twenty-three also says *'Above all else,
guard your heart, for everything you do flows from
it'*.

When I went back to my poem about blind
Bartimaeus after all those years, I found
something I had never seen before. It was when
Bartimaeus was asked a question by Jesus. The
question was *'What do you want me to do for
you?'* (Mark chapter ten, verse fifty-one). A very
strange question to a blind man from someone
who could give sight to the blind. But I felt this
question was being asked of me: 'Helene, what do
you want Me to do for you?' I could have given all
the right religious answers, but I didn't.

A few months later when visiting New Day
Community Church in South Carolina where
friends of mine, Stephanie and Scott Jones are
the pastors, I found that the answer came to me
without any processing of reasoning: 'Father, I
want a light spirit'. This is what I want, and I am
now beginning to live in it.

There has been a voice calling me to enter into the beauty of life that is free and open to everyone. To simply enter in and be part of it.

The calling of the voice, which I am beginning to recognise as the voice of my heavenly Father, is dawning on me to get as near to the heart of the world as I can. C. S. Lewis, a British writer and a lay theologian, born in 1898 in Belfast, said something that has grabbed my heart: 'The sweetest thing in all my life has been the longing to find the place where all the beauty came from.'

I believe that the world has a movement, the movement of the Holy Spirit, and it is a flowing movement because everything is going somewhere. Nothing stands still. All of this movement has a music, and a rhythm, and a song. Even the stars go streaming through space because of this movement. But in a very busy world a question arises 'do we hear the still small voice?'

A deep understanding has begun to grow inside of me, that this is my Father's world, and I belong. The beginning of finding a connection with nature soothes my body and soul. When I enter into this place of connection it becomes holy and divine, a place where I might see God. For me it is a place apart, a place of being alone, but not one of loneliness. Instead, a place of quiet. A place so still that you can tune into the rhythm that is all around us, and which invites us into a place of harmony with the whole of the Godhead, the Godhead who is ever present.

All of this is the wonderful gift of our Father's grace and love for us. I have come to understand that grace is not something we ask to come into our lives, it is something we find is here already, available within us.

We don't start to worship, we join in with what is going on around us all the time, because we can find God everywhere if we look.

So, as we see the heartache in the world today, may we still see the beauty of life, and not waste our time and energy criticising and arguing about what is right and wrong, what is good and bad, who is in and who is out, eating from the tree of the knowledge of good and evil rather from the tree of life which we find in Genesis chapter two, verse nine. It is a dualistic way of thinking and leads to boring Christianity where we live by rules and regulations.

As we begin to eat from the tree of life, we find that we are living a life of worship, and we begin to come into a spacious place.

The Ten Commandments are not a list of do's and don'ts. It is as if our Father is saying. 'I don't do these things and if you want to be like Me…..'

There is a beauty in all of life, and if we have eyes to see it, it causes us to live a life of worship, and we begin to come into a wide spacious place where we can breathe.

Why? Because life has a way of beating out the joy and wonder of living. You get talked about behind your back, you pour out time and energy, and even money, into something, and it explodes in your face.

You experience loss, disappointment, being let down, you lose something or someone, and a hardness can begin to cover your heart. You become more tired and exhausted and think, 'why will I stick my neck out once more and get shot down again?' In contrast though, we are called to taste and see that God is good (Psalm thirty-four, verse eight), and this involves all of our senses.

As I said earlier, I believe that spiritual things need to be tasted before they are understood and this brings us deeper into an awareness of God who is. He is as close to us as our breath: Genesis chapter two, verse seven: *'Then the Lord God formed a man from the dust of the ground and breathed into his nostrils the breath of life, and the man became a living being.'*

The Father invites us to 'change and become like little children (Mathew chapter eighteen, verse three). A child is open to awe and wonder and in order for us to begin to experience this awe and wonder perhaps we need to come to the end of our human resources or our grown-up-ness, before we discover how generous, kind and powerful is our God.

- Mother Teresa was a Catholic nun who worked with the homeless, the poor and the lepers in Calcutta. She said 'the only success is faithfulness'. To be faithful to this inner love is in itself the greatest success.'

As we begin to be awakened, we find that we are participating in something bigger than ourselves. We begin to live in the gift of life that has been given to us.

- John O'Donaghue, an Irish poet/priest, who I mentioned earlier, said this, which I love:

> 'On the day when the weight deepens on your shoulders and you stumble and fall, may the clay dance to balance you. And when your eyes freeze behind the grey window and the ghost of loss gets into you, may a flock of colours, indigo, red, green and azure blue, come to awaken in you a meadow of delight.
>
> When the canvas frays in the curragh of thought and a stain of ocean blackens beneath you, may there come across the waters a path of yellow moonlight to bring you safely home.'

As we begin to see the beauty all around we lose our desire to judge and criticise. Why? Because judgement saps our energy and strength. We begin to experience the gift of God, even in His seeming absence, more deeply than we can ever possibly imagine.

As I get older, I have come to ponder that in order for us to die well, we need to live well. My prayer is that I won't die without having lived. Why? Because life is a gift.

In the book of Ecclesiastes in chapter three, verses one to six, we read:

> '*There is a time for everything, and a season for every activity under the heavens: a time to be born and a time to die, a time to plant and a time to uproot, a time to kill and a time to heal, a time to tear down and a time to build, a time to weep and a time to laugh, a time to mourn and a time to dance, a time to scatter stones and a time to gather them, a time to embrace and a time to refrain from embracing, a time to search and a time to give up, a time to keep and a time to throw away.*'

My understanding of this is that deep inside every human heart there is an ache. We don't like to face the ache. We try to drown it out with all sorts of things but it is still there. When we have that ache it nudges us to accept our humanity, and when we accept our humanity we can begin to move into freedom, because it is the ache within us that draws us to admit our need of God.

Could it be that we can become friends with the inevitability of our own death? If so, it can help us to celebrate the eternity of our own soul which death cannot ever touch.

James Jordan said 'knowing everything does not make you happy'. So often we journey through life with the eyes of our heart that are not fully open, and my longing is for a greater insight to see more deeply into His wonders, because, as it says in Genesis chapter one many times '*He looked at all He had made and it was good*'. It is interesting to note that God did not say everything He had made was perfect. He said it was 'good'. If something is perfect it is static and has no room for change or movement or re-shaping or reforming.

In Matthew chapter five, verse forty-eight it says '*be perfect, therefore, as your heavenly Father is perfect*'. However, the real meaning in this is 'to be whole' as your heavenly Father is whole.

I am coming to understand that His Presence is in all things and my longing is to find Him in all things that are living. His very breath pulsates through everything.

St Cuthbert, born in 634 AD, was known as the fire of the north, a saint in the early Northumbrian church in the Celtic tradition. He said 'One thing influences another. If a spider's web which is attached to a tree trembles, its tremors are felt by the tree, the roots and the very earth. A person who was sensitive enough to the earth would feel those vibrations.'

- Richard Rohr, a Franciscan priest, says 'Our goal is to help us live before we die, so we are ready for real life'. He goes on to say 'The amazing thing is that my life is not about me, I am about life'.

- Abraham Joshua Heschel says 'above all (and here I am thinking of the young) let them remember to build their life as a work of art.'

I personally believe that wherever there is art, beauty and creativity, there is the presence of God. Why do I think that? It is because He is the source of all these things. He is the Creator.

We will never live from our true selves until we have peace with who we really are as His sons and daughters, sons and daughters of the Father.

As I have laid out my ponderings and meditations I close with two thoughts which I would like to live by and be known for. I am not there yet and perhaps never will be, but the only way is to grow in this.

Firstly, I will not try harder but will just accept that I am accepted.

Secondly, I am beginning to come into a greater awakening that I am a beloved son of Almighty God.

CHAMPION LAKES B.C.
JUL 2022

Grace and peace to you.

Enjoy the journey. THX HELENE, I WILL

READING THIS SLOWLY, WITH
YOUR OWN MARKER, WHERE BY
YOU HILITE THAT WHICH TOUCHED
YOUR HEART. YOU WILL KNOW IT AS
IT HAPPENS. OFTEN WHEN MY HEART IS
BURDENED AND HARD, DARK PERHAPS
AND NOTHING SEEMS TO PENETRATE
THAT IS WHEN I MOST NEED TO
REMEMBER, I AM ABOUT LIFE... DISCOVER
LIVING, BREETHING.. AND RENEWING
MY SOUL, BODY - WITHIN GODS
FIRST BOOK. LIKE A PERFECT FATHER
WOULD, HE HAS MADE A UNIVERSE
THAT SCREAMS, "ITS FOOD, COME SEE,
COME TASTE OF ITS GOODNESS"
AS I DO, LIGHT COMES IN, AND
WORDS SUCH AS WRITTEN HERE
BY HELENE, (AND THE WORDS SHE
READ AND PASSED ALONG), SING TO
MY BEING. SO MANY LET US KNOW
OF THESE SABATICALS, OH HOW WE
TAKE HEART WHEN WE R

BR